MILL, MU
AND
RAILWAY

The Story of Gibson Mill;
the Hawden Hole Murder;
and the Hardcastle Crags Railway

by

PETER THOMAS

ISBN 0 9535405 0 2
© Peter Thomas
Published by Peter Thomas
Printed by Airedale Print, Halifax

First published 1973.
Revised edition 1999.

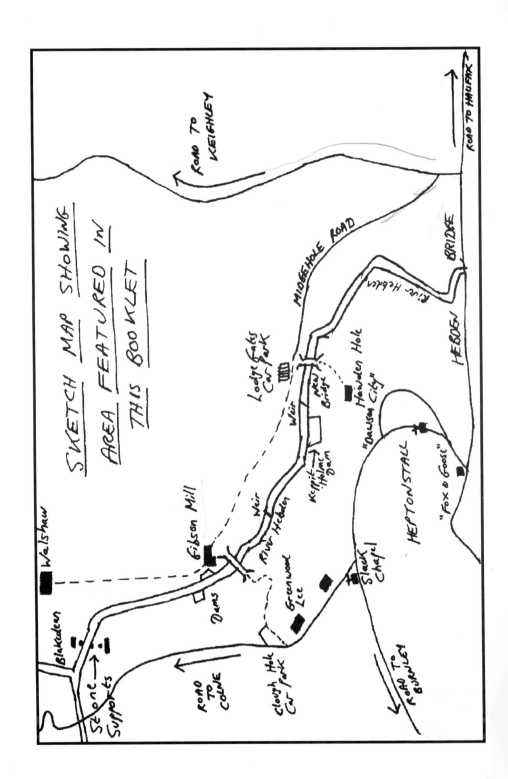

PREFACE

The 'Mill' section of this booklet tells the story of a central landmark in Hardcastle Crags, Gibson Mill, and something of the family whose name it carries. It is very much a 'flesh and blood' story of a little luck, a lot of hard work, and the creation of a little industrial empire in the heart of a rural beauty spot, with the Industrial Revolution as a backcloth. The Gibsons left an extraordinary physical legacy in the shape of Gibson Mill, the interior of Heptonstall Parish Church, and Greenwood Lee, which was the family home for many generations. All these features and connections will be explored in order to show how this family left its stamp on the immediate vicinity in a way that the Crossleys, on a grander scale, did around Halifax.

The 'Murder' section is concerned with a violent and fatal incident which took place in 1817, at Hawden Hole, at a time when Gibson Mill would have been in 'full cry'. Hawden Hole is to be found quite close to the Lodge Gates, at the bottom of the Crags. Although the present structure is a different one, parts of the old Hawden Hole are built into it, and one feature still remains that played a sinister part in the story - the old yew tree in the grounds.

The 'Railway' section details the rather astonishing story of a railway running up Hardcastle Crags at the beginning of the twentieth century. Such an unlikely scenario was occasioned by the building of reservoirs on the moors above the Crags, and resulted in the descent of the dreaded 'navvies' on the neighbourhood. Little evidence is left in the lower part of the Crags, but a trip to Blakedean will reveal a rather impressive memorial to the old line.

The best way to use this booklet is to make the Clough Hole car park, on the road to Widdop and Colne, a starting point. Greenwood Lee is close by, and the descent by footpath to Gibson Mill is about a half-a-mile. Much of what this booklet book has to say could be encompassed in this short walk alone.

If you want to be a little more ambitious, the section entitled 'A Stroll down the River' is just that, but entails a trip of about 1¼ miles and, of course, the return! However, there is much to be seen of interest, and the stroll ends at Hawden Hole, the next section of the booklet. There are, of course, various points in and around the Crags to which you could drive, and approach Hawden Hole on foot by a shorter route.

The trip to Blakedean to see the traces of the old railway is easily accomplished by car, although those with iron in their souls might wish to slog their way by foot up the valley from Gibson Mill, the best part of two miles. Finally, perhaps Heptonstall might be a calling point on the way home, to seek out the Gibson connection.

Hardcastle Crags is a beautiful spot, but it is also an industrial 'book' waiting to be read. I hope that you enjoy reading that 'book' as much as I have enjoyed writing this one.

Peter Thomas

GIBSON MILL

Most visitors to Hardcastle Crags are familiar with Gibson Mill, set deep within the beautiful woodlands of the River Hebden. Many may wonder at industrialisation having once intruded into such a rural setting, but the deep, wooded valleys of Calderdale have many such examples of our early industrial heritage, which began in such spots of tranquil beauty. This was due to the priceless asset of water power to drive water wheels.

Not many industrial remains, however, are in such complete condition as Gibson Mill. The main reason for this is that the mill has adopted several different identities since it closed as a working factory around 1900, and this has helped in its preservation. Visitors, then, may wonder about the history of Gibson Mill. When was it working? What did it produce? Who owned it? What was it like to work there? This book is an attempt to answer these questions, as well as to sketch in some of the surprising and enterprising ventures the mill has been the subject of since the end of its 'working' life.

To begin with, the first question which might spring to any visitor's mind. Did someone called Gibson own Gibson Mill? Indeed he did. The Gibson family was an ancient and well-known family in the district, and their home was Greenwood Lee.

Greenwood Lee

Early Days - Greenwood Lee is situated on the right-hand side of the road running from Heptonstall Slack to Blakedean (old road to Colne) shortly before Clough Hole car-park, which overlooks Hardcastle Crags. The name of this well-preserved and beautiful building is taken from the ancient settlement of 'Greenwood' which covered much of this hillside above the River Hebden. 'Greenwood' is one of the oldest sites in Calderdale, and was probably settled on in Saxon times. However, it is not until Norman times that we have any human evidence, in the shape of one Wyomarus.

The First Greenwoods - In 1154 Wyomarus established his home on this site, and adopted a surname - Wyomarus de Greenwode - thus founding a very common local name. Ask any genuine 'local' about his or her ancestry, and the name of 'Greenwood' is almost sure to feature somewhere. Indeed, the Society of Greenwoods of America contends that all Greenwoods are descended from Wyomarus de Greenwode.

The name was mentioned in the Poll Tax returns for 1379, both 'Richard de Grenewod' and 'Thomas de Grenewod' appearing as payers of the tax. However, the first mention of someone indisputably connected with the homestead of Greenwood Lee comes in 1439, in the reign of Henry

Greenwood Lee, the Gibson home for many generations

VI. The Rental of Halifax, made by the Court of Manor of Halifax in this year, recorded that, '*John of Grenewodde, of Grenewodlee, holds the lands and tenements called Grenewodlee, and pays rent yearly at 6s. 7½d...*'. Later, one Thomas Greenwood of Greenwood Lee, took his seat as a juror at the Lord's Court held at Halifax on October 17th 1513.

The Building Takes Shape 1657 - 1762 - Greenwood Lee passed out of the hands of the Greenwood family in 1657 when the residence, along with the estates attached to it, were sold by Robert Greenwood to one John Ramsden of Haworth. Most of the existing structure of the house was probably built in the seventeenth century, although the barn is certainly much older. In 1710 Greenwood Lee came into the possession of a Mr William Sutcliffe (incidentally another very common local surname). The mark of this family can still be found at Greenwood Lee, for above the porch is the following inscription in stone:-

R.G.S
Robert and
Grace Sut
cliffe 1712

Robert was the second son of William Sutcliffe. In 1744, Robert's son, John, died in financial difficulties, and the estate of Greenwood Lee was held in mortgage until it was sold by auction in 1762.

The Befuddled Buy - Now at last the Gibsons, after whom Gibson Mill was named, come into our story. At the auction of 1762, Greenwood Lee and its estate was purchased by one Abraham Gibson, and local rumour has it that he was drunk at the auction and not quite aware of what he was doing. Certainly by all accounts he was surprised to learn, 'the morning after the night before', that he had bought Greenwood Lee. Like it or not, the property was his, and Abraham set out to make the best of it, one method of recouping his outlay being by the sale of timber from his estate.

The Building Earns its Keep - Like many other farmers - cum - gentry in the district, the Gibsons were involved part-time in the staple industry of the area, textiles. During the eighteenth century, Greenwood Lee itself was used for spinning cotton. A water-wheel was inserted into the building by cutting away part of the upper floor, and water was conveyed straight down the yard by conduit to the wheel, which drove *'spinning jennies'* (invented around 1765) in the upper rooms.

The first Abraham Gibson of Greenwood Lee died in 1780, leaving the estate to his son, also named Abraham. At around the turn of the century, the textile industry was in a transitional stage, changing from a domestic-based one to a factory-based one. The second Abraham Gibson must have decided to move with the times, and involve himself in the cotton industry in a bigger way, for in 1800 Gibson Mill (at first called Lord Holme Mill) was built in Hardcastle Crags. At this point the 'spinning jennies' were transferred from Greenwood Lee to Gibson Mill

Greenwood Lee and the later Gibsons - The second Abraham Gibson had several children. His eldest son, however, yet another Abraham, had an unfortunate accident and was killed in 1805 by a fall from a horse whilst returning from Manchester. The estate passed to the second son, William.

William Gibson was the father of another Abraham (the fourth of our story), who did not marry until late in life. He married Mary Elizabeth Mitchell of Boston Hill, Wadsworth, in 1886, and died in 1907 at the age of 80. The marriage produced the last of the Gibson line, our fifth Abraham, or 'Young Ab' as it is said he was popularly known. He served as a Private in the 1914-18 War, being in the Motor Transport Division of the Army Service Corps, before returning to enjoy quieter times in his inheritance of Greenwood Lee.

The last Abraham Gibson remained a bachelor and died in 1956. He was proud of the beauty of his estate in Hardcastle Crags, and he looked after it well. He was often to be seen at work repairing stepping stones, building seats and shelters, for he was anxious that the public should enjoy the beauty of his woodlands. He was angry whenever the public did damage, but his will after his death proved that he wished Hardcastle

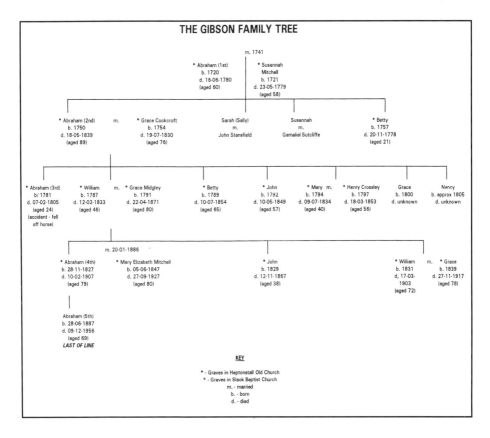

THE GIBSON FAMILY TREE

m. 1741

* Abraham (1st) b. 1720 d. 16-06-1780 (aged 60) — * Susannah Mitchell b. 1721 d. 23-05-1779 (aged 58)

* Abraham (2nd) b. 1750 d. 18-05-1839 (aged 89) m. * Grace Cockcroft b. 1754 d. 19-07-1830 (aged 76)

Sarah (Sally) m. John Stansfield

Susannah m. Gamaliel Sutcliffe

* Betty b. 1757 d. 20-11-1778 (aged 21)

* Abraham (3rd) b/ 1781 d. 07-02-1805 (aged 24) (accident - fell off horse)

* William b. 1787 d. 12-02-1833 (aged 46) m. * Grace Midgley b. 1791 d. 22-04-1871 (aged 80)

* Betty b. 1789 d. 10-07-1854 (aged 65)

* John b. 1792 d. 10-05-1849 (aged 57)

° Mary m. b. 1794 d. 09-07-1834 (aged 40)

° Henry Crossley b. 1797 d. 18-03-1853 (aged 56)

Grace b. 1800 d. unknown

Nancy b. approx 1805 d. unknown

m. 20-01-1886

* Abraham (4th) b. 28-11-1827 d. 10-02-1907 (aged 79)

* Mary Elizabeth Mitchell b. 05-06-1847 d. 27-09-1927 (aged 80)

* John b. 1829 d. 12-11-1867 (aged 38)

* William b. 1831 d. 17-03-1903 (aged 72) m. * Grace b. 1839 d. 27-11-1917 (aged 78)

Abraham (5th) b. 28-06-1887 d. 09-12-1956 (aged 69) *LAST OF LINE*

KEY

* - Graves in Heptonstall Old Church
° - Graves in Slack Baptist Church
m. - married
b. - born
d. - died

Crags to remain a place open to public use and enjoyment.

Abraham Gibson's will stated that the National Trust should inherit the family home, Greenwood Lee; the woodland part of his Hardcastle Crags estate, amounting to 37 acres on the left bank of the stream as one looks up it; and Gibson Mill, plus several farms and cottages. He also left a bequest of £10,000 to Heptonstall Parish Church (where many members of the family are buried), and the residue of the Gibson Estate, after death duties and funeral expenses, was to go to the Church.

The woodland given to the National Trust in Abraham Gibson's will more or less linked up with the land given to the Trust in 1950 by Henry Mitchell Ingham at the upper, Blakedean end of the valley, and the pine woodland on the other side of the river, given to the National Trust in 1948 by Lord Savile. The Trust decided that it did not want Greenwood Lee, and other farms and cottages, as no money had been set aside in the will for their maintenance. Therefore they were sold by auction, and the money received went into the residue of the estate earmarked for Heptonstall Parish Church, which eventually benefited to the tune of £40,000 or so.

Heptonstall - The Gibson Connection

HEBDEN BRIDGE LIT. & SCI. SOCIETY; AT 616.
A nineteenth century view of St. Thomas à Becket - still roofed

Heptonstall is worth a visit at any time, but it is particularly worth pursuing the Gibson connection with the village, which goes back for many hundreds of years. The first calling point is the old church of St Thomas à Becket.

For at least three hundred and fifty years, Gibsons were buried at Heptonstall, and their gravestones are sprinkled about the peaceful interior of the old church. On sunny afternoons the passage of time is marked by the changes of light and shade which angle across the gravestones on the floor. Every gravestone tells a story. Perhaps we have just turned back the corner of one page. The rest lies hidden - 'between the lines'.

The earliest gravestone is hard to decipher, but it can be picked out, about eight or nine paces in from the door.

'Elizabeth, daughter of John Gibson of Langfield, who departed this life the 23rd March 1601'

We know that in 1714, an early Abraham Gibson had his full name inscribed on his pew door in the North gallery

Gibsons at rest - Heptonstall Old Church

of the old church. The family's progress to prominence after this date is measured in part by the inscriptions which lie beneath our feet throughout the interior of the old church - six stones in all - the names of them being indicated on the Family Tree on page 7.

A walk up to the new church will further confirm the importance of the Gibsons to Heptonstall. If one enters by the main door and turns right, the Gibson link is clearly visible in the shape of two tablets on the rear wall. The top one indicates the strength of the family's connection with the old church, for originally it was placed there

The end of the connection is expressed in the bottom slate tablet, which is a simple memorial to the legacy which the last Abraham Gibson left to the parish church in 1956. A far grander memorial is the interior of the church itself. Abraham Gibson's bequest was to be used to provide memorial stones or tablets; or for the provision of altars, altar rails, pews, windows, church bells or other vessels, ornaments or furniture; or for the improvement of the Church or Sunday School, *'to the memory of my father, Abraham Gibson ... and also of my mother, Mary Elizabeth Gibson ...'*

In the event, a sum of money was released which allowed just about all of this to be done within the following ten years. The new Parish Church Hall is to be found on the lane which runs along the top side of the churchyard, towards the new graveyard. A stone is inscribed, *'through the bequest of the late Abraham Gibson 1963'.*

Side by side in the churchyard - 'ancient and modern'

However, the modernised interior of the new church is the most striking evidence of Abraham Gibson's bequest. Inevitably, the major changes did not please everyone, and there was much controversy, and not a little bitterness at the time, concerning the way his money was being spent. Nevertheless, the interior of the new church is, in its way, as impressive a memorial to the Gibson family as benefactors, as is Gibson Mill to the family as business entrepreneurs.

The Beginnings of Gibson Mill

Gibson Mill dominates the valley, impressive in its idyllic setting. However, no matter how aesthetic the location, Gibson Mill was built for one reason - to make use of water power to drive cotton spinning machinery for profit - and much of the wealth of the Gibson family was generated from this source.

From about the mid-eighteenth century, the Industrial Revolution transformed the face of Britain and the lives of its people. Particularly in the North and the Midlands, Britain became a land of mills and mines, the veritable 'workshop of the world' by 1850. Britain's industrial prosperity was based on coal, iron and above all, cotton. Now we usually associate Yorkshire with wool and Lancashire with cotton, and certainly there was a strong domestic woollen industry in the Halifax area, with hand-loom weavers grinding out a living from the land and the loom. The Western end of the Calder Valley, however, was close enough to Lancashire to be influenced by changes in the cotton industry there, and changes there were a plenty around 1800!

From the invention of Kay's *flying shuttle* in 1733 to the advent of Cartwright's *power loom* in 1784, a series of inventions revolutionised the spinning and weaving of cotton. The ultimate result was the concentration of the industry in factories, and the extinction of the domestic industry. The hand-loom weavers fought hard. It is estimated that as late as 1830 there were still about 200,000 hand loom weavers at work in the cotton industry, and the last hand-loom weaver in Heptonstall died only in 1902, but their fate was sealed. If cotton was to be 'king', it ruled from the factory place and not the fireplace!

And what of the Gibsons of Greenwood Lee, farming the thin soils of the Pennine borderlands between Lancashire and Yorkshire? They too were involved in textiles to supplement their farming, and we have already seen that a water wheel had been inserted into Greenwood Lee to drive 'spinning jennies' in the upper rooms. It is against all this background of the Industrial Revolution that Lord Holme Mill (Gibson Mill) was built around 1800, and the machinery transferred from Greenwood Lee, as the second Abraham Gibson decided to enter the cotton industry in a bigger way, making use of the driving force of the River Hebden.

Gibson Mill - industry in a rural setting

The capital required for such a venture suggests that the Gibsons were gentleman farmers at least, with an eye to expanding markets. Factory production of course needs a good transport system for the carriage of both raw materials and finished goods. Perhaps it was no accident that Gibson Mill was built only two years after the opening of the Hebden Bridge stretch of the Rochdale Canal, an event which was to link the locality with all the growing industrial regions and centres of the North, not least with the thriving cotton importing city of Liverpool.

Life at Gibson Mill

In 1833 the Factories Inquiries Commission visited Gibson Mill as part of its wider search into factory conditions, and its report furnishes an interesting picture of life at Gibson Mill.

Power was provided by a five-horse-power wheel fed by the River Hebden. At this time there was only one lodge or dam, situated immediately behind the mill (the second and larger dam, a little upstream, was built later). At times of drought work began earlier and finished later at the mill, probably because difficulties in water supply to the wheel made it take longer to get through what was considered a sufficient day's work.

In 1833 Gibson Mill employed 21 workers paid by the hour, and one piece worker. A normal week's work was 72 hours. On weekdays work began at 6am and finished at 7.30pm; on Saturdays 9½ hours were worked. On weekdays there were two stoppages, one of 20 minutes for breakfast, another of 40 minutes for dinner. The Saturday stoppage is not recorded. The report was careful to point out that during both the breakfast and dinner breaks the machinery was stopped, for this was a luxury not always enjoyed in some factories at that time, where food and drink had to be snatched wherever possible while the machines ground remorselessly on.

If any worker lost any time it was made up by working an extra half hour at the end of the day, or by a cut in wages. There was no sickness pay, but sometimes there was pay after accidents (again a generous provision compared with some mills of the time). As for holidays, two days paid holiday were enjoyed at Christmas. There were several other unpaid holiday such as Shrove Tuesday, Whitsuntide and for fairs.

What a huge gulf opens up, then, between working hours and conditions now for the ordinary working person, and those which existed around 1833. Imagine the scene at shortly before 6am on a weekday morning as the clatter of clogs heralded the arrival of workers from the local hamlets. The workers would rarely see daylight in winter, rising before dawn and finishing after dusk. There would be little chance to admire the beauties of Hardcastle Crags. Summers, of course, would be more bearable, but in times of drought the day's work would be even longer. Summer or winter days would be long and hard, with little or no security against sickness, accident and old age. The few holidays would be greeted with real joy, and perhaps hearty revelling.

The gulf widens even further when one considers who actually did the work, and the wages they received. In 1833 the Gaukrogers, then renting the mill from the Gibsons, stated that *children from ten to sixteen years were best for their work*. Therefore, at an age range which roughly corresponds to secondary school age today, children were working a normal week of 72 hours at Gibson Mill. Also, at an age which today is the minimum one for even starting full-time work, factory children of 1833 were being regarded as slight less 'useful'.

Why was this so? Partly the answer lies in the fact that children were small and nimble, able to get under and among the machines to clean up cotton waste or tie up broken threads. They were small and nimble enough to do this while the machinery was in motion (even though horrific accidents sometimes did occur through sheer fatigue) and so production need not stop. However, the most priceless advantage of employing children was that they cost much less, and the same applied to women.

Machines had taken the craft and skill out of spinning as it had been practised at home, and the work in factories could be done easily by unskilled women and children.

The following chart shows the ages and wages of workers at Gibson Mill in 1833:-

Age	No. of males	No.of females	Wage per week	
10-12 years	1	2	2/6d	(12½p)
12-14 years	0	3	3/-	(15p)
14-16 years	0	1	4/-	(20p)
16-18 years	1	2	4/6d	(22½p)
18-21 years	0	3	6/6d	(32½p)
Over 21 years	3	6	males 17/-	(85p)
			females 6/6d	(32½p)

Notice the advantage in cost in employing workers below the age of 21 years. Even workers over the age of 21 years were more often women, as they were paid less. Among the young, girls were employed more than boys. Adult males were in low demand, and this could cause hardship and unemployment.

These, then, were certainly the 'bad old days', but at least Gibson Mill seems to have escaped the worst excesses of the time. Reports from factories elsewhere speak of children as young as five and six being employed, and when the mills were 'thrang' (busy) at certain times of the year, children having to start work as early as 4 or 5am, and working late into the night. It has been estimated that a child following a spinning machine could walk twenty miles in twelve hours. Little wonder that many children went home too tired to eat.

What a relief, then, to read in the 1833 report that the tenants of Lord Holme Mill made a point of stating that there was no corporal punishment in their mill. This was not the case everywhere, for in some mills men were employed to keep exhausted children awake with the strap!

By the standards of the time, then, and on the evidence given to the Factories Enquiries Commission of 1833, the Gaukrogers at Gibson Mill seem to have been reasonable employers. Their hours of work were not excessive for the time, and at least they allowed proper meal breaks, with the machinery stopped, and refrained from having their young workers physically abused in order to keep up the work rate. On the other hand, they could not be described as 'enlightened', for in their comments to the report of 1833 they joined in the general lament of the manufacturers of the time to the effect that Ashley's Bill would ruin them. What was this terribl**e** Ashley's Bill? It was simply a movement among reforming MPs, and a few enlightened mill-owners, to limit by law the number of hours worked daily by women and young persons to *TEN*.

The man leading the campaign was Anthony Ashley Cooper, later Lord Shaftesbury who dedicated his life to a series of good causes. A strong local champion of the bill was 'Honest' John Fielden of Todmorden, whose mills were examples of humanity. But the clamour from most mill-owners, echoed at Gibson Mill, was almost deafening. They claimed that shorter hours would increase costs of production, resulting in a fall in demand, and thus unemployment. As the great radical, Cobbett, sarcastically observed, the entire industrial welfare of England seemed to rest upon, *'30,000 little girls. If these little girls worked two hours a day less, our manufacturing supremacy would depart from us'*. In fact, the opposition to the bill was strong enough to delay its passing until 1847, when the Ten Hours Act did indeed limit the work of women to ten hours per day, thus (theoretically) doing the same for men, for factories could not operate at all without the women and children.

We must view life at Gibson Mill, then, in the context of the early nineteenth century, hard times when men and women were struggling to achieve reasonable working conditions and decent living standards against manufacturers who were strongly represented in Parliament. It is not a happy picture, but at least the workers at Gibson Mill lived and worked in a beautiful, rural setting. They did not have to face the rigours of factory life in an urban setting, where huge and gloomy factories were set amidst the disease-ridden slums which were beginning to blight our great northern cities.

A Brief Reconstruction of Gibson Mill

There cannot be many industrial remains which retain their original structure as fully and clearly as does Gibson Mill. Its industrial history passed on around 1900 leaving it, in a sense, 'high and dry'. Fortunately, however, only internal changes were needed to adapt the mill to a variety of new roles. Demolition, or radical external changes, were not necessary. Therefore it is possible, with a little guesswork, to look at the mill today and reconstruct it as a working textiles factory. Here visitors can indulge in a little 'detective' work.

The most interesting and visible 'clue' to be seen is when one is facing upstream and looking at the main wall of Gibson Mill over-looking the entrance yard. Towards the right-hand side, a straight seam of mortar runs up the stonework from bottom to top, as in the photograph opposite.

This indicates that an extension was built on to the mill. Look at the former workers' cottages to the right. The one nearest to the mill has a similar straight seam of mortar - again suggesting additional building work.

Returning to the mill wall, the question is which bit was added to which? Searching amongst records and maps can be fascinating and rewarding, for in this case it came up with the answer. An old map of 1833 of the Township of Heptonstall shows Gibson Mill as consisting only of the central block, and so anything to the right of the straight line seam was added later. Even the building attached to the central block on the

The straight seam; extensions to the mill

left, nearest the river, was not there in 1833. Therefore, when the factory commissioners visited Lord Holme (Gibson) Mill in 1833, they would have found a fairly small three storey building engaged in spinning 'cotton throstle twist' powered by a five-horse-power water wheel which was fed from the dam immediately at the rear.

The second interesting and visible 'clue' is now to be found by going to the rear. Skirt the right-hand side of the mill and follow the path at the back, between the rear wall and the dam. About three- quarters of the way along is a curved archway of stones at about ground level in the rear wall. This was the water entrance, and on working days in 1833 water would have been pouring through to drive a water wheel which towered higher than the ground floor. Within this section of the mill is a long and narrow room, reaching from front to back, which housed the water wheel, and which rises to the height of the ceiling above the first floor, in other words two storeys high. The curved archway of stones was the roof of the water entrance, but at a later date the space between the dam wall and the mill was concrete, thus blocking off this entrance. (Notice the metal grill set inside the outer dam wall. Reference is made to this in the section entitled 'Gibson Mill in the Twentieth Century'.) When the water had finished its work of driving spinning machines, it left the front of the mill by means of a drain which ran underground down the yard, and on into the River Hebden. The exit of this drain can still be seen as a tunnel running into the river about 50 yards below the stepping stones -another 'clue'.

But what evidence have we as to *why* and *when* extensions were made to Gibson Mill? The *why* is perhaps not too difficult. At some point after 1833 steam power was introduced to Gibson Mill, and the new building to the right of the straight mortar seam represents the addition of an engine house, a boiler pit and a chimney to accommodate the new source of power. The furthest extension to the right has all the appearance of being constructed to house a boiler, for it is little more than a pit, sunk below the level of the rest of the mill, and with a roof sloping up towards the chimney. Possibly the building nearest the river, to the left of the central block, was also added at the same time.

The question of *when* this change took place is not so easy to solve. The building itself surrenders no clues. As we have seen, the Factories Inquiries Commission of 1833 makes mention only of a water wheel at Gibson Mill, so steam power must have come to the mill later than this. Between 1840 and 1861 the Gibson family leased the mill to the Gaukrogers, and it seems unlikely that tenants would introduce such sweeping changes. Therefore, there is a strong possibility that steam power was introduced after 1861, when the Gibsons began to work the mill for themselves again.

There is an equally strong chance that the first *weaving* was introduced to Gibson Mill along with steam power, to add to the spinning operations. Certainly the range of activities was expanding, for a West Riding Directory of 1861 lists Gibson Bros. for the first time as cotton and

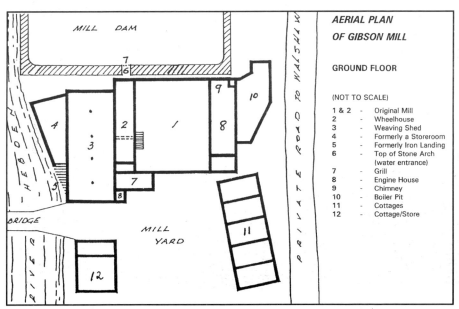

AERIAL PLAN

OF GIBSON MILL

GROUND FLOOR

(NOT TO SCALE)

1 & 2 - Original Mill
2 - Wheelhouse
3 - Weaving Shed
4 - Formerly a Storeroom
5 - Formerly Iron Landing
6 - Top of Stone Arch
(water entrance)
7 - Grill
8 - Engine House
9 - Chimney
10 - Boiler Pit
11 - Cottages
12 - Cottage/Store

MILL DAM

MILL YARD

BRIDGE

HEBDEN WATER

RIVER

worsted manufacturers of Lord Holme Mill, and later documents describe the mill as having a weaving shed. It is very likely, then, that all the extensions took place around 1861 to accommodate both steam power and weaving, and that the substantial building between the central block and the river was a weaving shed.

Power looms would be brought into this new shed, and perhaps throughout the ground floor, in which case the spinning machinery would have been transferred upstairs.

The water wheel, incidentally, need not have become immediately redundant. It could well have been retained, for a while at least, as an auxiliary to the steam engine. If operations were extending after 1861, demand for water could have been so great that perhaps it was at this time that the second dam was built further upstream.

One vital element is missing in this reconstruction of Gibson Mill as a working concern - people - and these must be provided by the imagination. Let your mind's eye see a busy working day in the 1860s, with the arrival of horses and carts heavily laden with coal, cotton or wool,

The old weaving shed; later a rolling-skating rink

and others departing with cloth. Clogs clatter across the cobbled yard as carters and warehouse workers labour and talk together, their words perhaps drowned by the constant, rhythmic clashing of the looms from within the mill.

An iron landing once rang above the river from the weaving shed to the store shed at the rear (now gone). Imagine a few weavers pausing to snatch a breath of fresh air on this landing, especially on a hot summer's day. In all probability the windows and doors of the mill would be kept tightly shut because humid conditions were best for spinning and weaving in order to lessen the chance of threads breaking. Therefore the workers would be glad to escape from the noise and the heat once in a while, to stand on the landing above the coolness of the river, and perhaps glance up to watch the smoke from Gibson Mill chimney idly curling away among the trees.

The end of Gibson Mill as a factory is somewhat shrouded in mystery. Kelly's Directory of the West Riding of Yorkshire, both for 1893 and 1897, makes mention of 'Abraham Gibson, weaver, Gibson Wood and New Bridge Mills', but a local Halifax directory for 1894 makes no mention of the Gibsons as manufacturers. Interestingly, it is recorded in 1894 that Abraham Gibson deposited title deeds as securities to secure a loan from the Halifax Commercial Banking Company Ltd. Was this due to financial difficulties or plans for expansion into another field? Whatever the answer, Gibson Mill was closed down as a textile factory sometime between 1897 and 1901, and the noise of industry was stilled in this part of the valley. However, Gibson Mill was far from finished, and as we shall see next, the noises of leisure as opposed to labour filled the woodlands as it played its different roles in the twentieth century.

Gibson Mill in the Twentieth Century

As we have seen, as a manufacturing concern Gibson Mill closed down sometime between 1897 and 1901, but enterprising minds were at work! The rise of cheap public transport brought with it the rise of the 'pleasure' industry, and the age of the 'day tripper' had dawned. Foreign holidays were still the preserve of a wealthy few, but at least on holidays and at weekends ordinary working people could board a train and leave the noise and dirt of their towns and cities in search of the countryside.

Hardcastle Crags provided just such a retreat for thousands of visitors from Lancashire and Yorkshire. Visitors flocked to the Crags to enjoy the simple pleasures of walking, paddling and picnicking in an age where pleasures and entertainments for working people were few. These visitors, of course, would become hungry and thirsty. If Gibson Mill no longer paid its way as a textiles mill, why should it not adapt to changing times, and pay its way in the catering field?

18

The 'Fun Palace' - Therefore, the first of the many changes of role took place at Gibson Mill which enabled the building to preserve its essential character intact as an example of an early water-powered cotton spinning mill. *'The Hebden Bridge Times and Gazette'* for March 28th 1902

Gibson Mill as part of the leisure industry - about 1910

states that the buildings at Gibson Mill were about to be transformed into an elaborate dining saloon. Also, a document dated November 2nd 1918 relates to the release of a mortgage taken out in 1902. The mortgage debt was worth £4,260, and was taken out by Abraham Gibson and son on property which included Greenwood Lee and *'all that Mill or Factory heretofore Cotton Factory called Lord Holme Mill or Gibson Mill with the weaving shed, warehouse, cottages, engine house and other building thereto adjoining or belonging, but which mill ... has been for a long time disused and used only as Refreshment rooms in the Summer season'*. No doubt the mortgage taken out in 1902 was for the purpose of converting the mill into a dining saloon.

Very soon, then, Gibson Mill could offer itself as an admirable and spacious catering establishment. The Gibsons did not run the catering themselves but leased the property to various proprietors. Thus we find in Robinson's Halifax and District Directory for 1905-6, '*Lord Holme Restaurant, Hardcastle Crags. (Proprietor: W. Shackleton)*'.

Ambitious proprietors launched into other schemes to provide dancing and roller-skating. There was boating on the dam, and swing-boats on the grass further down the river. Before the 1939-1945 War, a sign advertising the 'Fun Palace' was located at the junction of Widdop Road and the track leading down to Gibson Mill (near the modern car-park). It read, '*Lord Holme Refreshment Room -skating, dancing, catering. Accommodation for 600*'.

Large-scale catering and dancing at Gibson Mill declined after the Second World War, along with the number of visitors to the Crags. The coming of the motor-car meant that people were able to go further afield for their relaxation, and the variety of recreations became much greater for people. Nevertheless a café operated from one of the adjoining cottages for many years, and one entertainment which did last into the early 1950s was roller-skating. From the early years of this century, roller- skating was tremendously popular, not only at Gibson Mill, but throughout the country as a whole. At Gibson Mill, roller-skaters displayed their skills in the old weaving shed, which had handy pillars down the centre to support the less skilful!

'Young Ab' - Throughout all these carnival years of Gibson Mill, the last Abraham Gibson retained more than a passing interest in what was going on. 'Young Ab' seems to have been quite a character. Two or three hundred yards downstream from Gibson Mill is a stretch of flat grassland on the right-hand bank as one descends. Here were to be found the swings and roundabouts of the 1920s and 1930s. Here also, if local rumour is to be believed, 'Young Ab', on holidays, ran a string of donkeys, as on the Blackpool sands.

He was quick to see other possibilities. Around 1930, when electric lighting was still a novelty in country areas, Abraham decided that Greenwood Lee should have it. He utilised the old wheel house and installed a turbine there using water from the dam. This was the time when the space between the back of the mill and the dam was concreted in, raising the level of the dam, and a metal grill was inserted in the inside of the dam wall to let water through to the turbine. The grill is still visible today. Electricity generated by the turbine was carried to Greenwood Lee by cables up the hillside.

Even today, if one stands on the bridge at Gibson Mill and looks away from the mill up the hillside towards Greenwood Lee, a slight thinning of the woodland shows where the cables once ran. How proudly Abraham must have sat in Greenwood Lee under probably the first electric light bulbs on the hillside. The cottages next to Gibson Mill were rented out as holiday cottages during the 1930s, and Abraham owned other cottages in the valley which he rented out. The occupiers also enjoyed the benefits of 'Gibson electricity', which was relayed to them. Apparently, however, the master switch was at Greenwood Lee, so that when Abraham went to bed everybody went to bed as the power was switched off!

Post-Gibson Days - After the death of the last Abraham Gibson in 1956, Gibson Mill and Hardcastle Crags passed into the hands of the National Trust by the terms of his will. Yet again the role of the mill changed, for in 1956 it was being rented by boy scouts from the Halifax area who had managed to repair the now disused turbine, and used it to provide light to the mill and adjoining cottages.

The scouting link remained in the 1970s, but since then Gibson Mill has stood empty and deserted, seemingly lacking a role. Fortunately, however, it has remained intact, and with the passage of time and the disappearance of industrial relics elsewhere, the almost unique nature of Gibson Mill has been recognised. There has been an awakening of interest in its possibilities. A few years ago the mill was chosen by a TV Company as ideal for a reconstruction of an early nineteenth century Luddite attack on a mill. The National Trust is engaged in implementing long-term plans for the mill as an environmental and exhibition centre, and there is every sign that Gibson Mill has at least one more role to play in the future.

A Stroll down the River

The Gibson family of Greenwood Lee either ran Gibson Mill themselves, or leased it to others, for the best part of the hundred years between 1800 and 1900. A Commercial Directory of 1828-9 lists Abraham Gibson and Sons, of Greenwood Lee, as cotton spinners and manufacturers. Another Directory, this time for 1861, lists Gibson Bros. as cotton and worsted manufacturers of Lord Holme Mill. However, in between time, the mill was leased for many years to another well-known local manufacturing family, James and Titus Gaukroger, who also owned a mill at New Bridge.

The journey down the river bank from Gibson Mill to the remains of New Bridge Mill, at the Lodge Gates, is about 1¼ miles. It is a naturalist's paradise, but it is also full of evidence of the impact of industrialisation on the valley. Following the left-hand bank of the River Hebden downstream for about three-quarters of a mile, the first clue is a weir across the river beyond the Hebden Hey Cub and Scout Hostel on the opposite bank. Notice the arch of the masonry, and how the weir is angled to force the flow of the water towards the right-hand bank, looking downstream. Here a *'goit'* (a channel or tunnel) took water ultimately to the water wheel at New Bridge Mill, but in stages which can be followed.

Just below the weir, the river sweeps along the base of a steep cliff of

The weir near Hebden Hey

shales and sandstones, clearly visible on the opposite bank. In the early nineteenth century, a tunnel was excavated behind this cliff face to continue the progress of the water from the weir. Walk a little further downstream, and you will need to climb above the river bank and descend again. As you do so, look carefully through the curtain of trees and you will see the cool, green waters of Keppit Holme dam on the opposite side of the river. This is easier to see in winter than in summer, but it was here that the water carried by the goit was stored.

From Keppit Holme dam, water was carried by goit right down to drive the water wheel at New Bridge Mill, assisted by yet another weir further downstream. Little remains of New Bridge Mill (in contrast to Gibson Mill) other than a mound of ivy covered ruins just near the Lodge Gates.

Cross the river via the bridge, and take the path which forks uphill to the right and find this rather melancholy heap of ruins. A further climb up the hillside brings you to Hawden Hole, the setting for another melancholy story, which will appear next in the booklet.

An old shot of New Bridge Mill as a tearoom

THE HAWDEN HOLE MURDER

Hawden Hole is now a fine restored property, which rejoices under the far grander name of *Hawdon Hall*. It can be found by crossing the bridge at the Lodge Gates to the right-hand bank of the river (looking downstream), and then taking the track through the woods up to the right, passing the ruins of New Bridge Mill. The track levels out at the junction with another track, and Hawden Hole stands a few yards along, below the level of the road.

The present property was not the old Hawden Hole, for the building itself has been demolished, although parts of it were built into the new structure. The old Hawden Hole stood at right-angles to the new building, which was then a barn, and much closer to the old yew tree which still stands in the grounds. This yew tree played a central part in a sinister story which took place in 1817, for it is said that two murderers hid in its branches before committing their crime.

HEBDEN BRIDGE LIT. & SCI. SOCIETY; AT 811

Hawden Hole and its yew tree - scene of a dark crime

On February 7th 1817, Samuel Sutcliffe, also known as 'Sammy o' Katty's', was strangled and robbed at Hawden Hole. The murderers, Michael Pickles, or 'Old Mike' as he was called, and John Greenwood, also known as 'Joan at Bog Eggs', were caught and hanged. Their arrest mainly revolved around a bank note.

At the time, several firms around Hebden Bridge issued private notes of varying values, and these were accepted and honoured just as bank notes are today. Among these firms was that of Mr John Sutcliffe of The Lee, which issued red cards valued at 3/6d.

The murder was committed on a Friday, and among the property taken from Hawden Hole was an unsigned note from Mytholm Mill. This note ensured that the murderers were not at liberty for long. For John Greenwood had a brother living at Luddenden named William, and John went to him and gave him the stolen

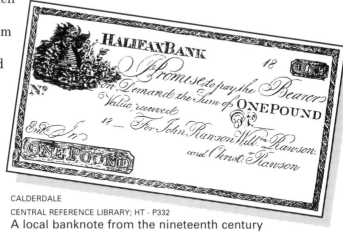

CALDERDALE
CENTRAL REFERENCE LIBRARY; HT - P332
A local banknote from the nineteenth century

unsigned note. This note now went on its travels in earnest, for William Greenwood went to the house of a Thomas Greenwood, of Birchcliffe, and bought a clock from him, partly paying him with the unsigned note. Thomas Greenwood then bought a chest of drawers from a Betty Wadsworth, paying her with the very same note. This was only Tuesday following the Friday on which the murder was committed, but the rapid circulation of the note now came to an abrupt halt.

Betty Wadsworth, the same evening she had received the note, attempted to buy groceries with it, but the grocer refused to accept the note because it was unsigned. Therefore, the following morning, Betty returned the note to Thomas Greenwood, complaining that it was not genuine.

Now, Thomas Greenwood was an illiterate weaver who worked for John Sutcliffe of The Lee. The day before, he had received a bank note from his employer as his wages, but not being able to read, Thomas did not know which was the note he had given to Betty, whether it was the note from his employer, or the note from William Greenwood.

Therefore Thomas went to see his employer at the Lee, and asked if he had given him an unsigned note by mistake the day before. Mr Sutcliffe had heard all about the unsigned note missing from the scene of the Hawden Hole Murder, and immediately sent for the constables. Meanwhile he learned from Thomas Greenwood that the source of the note was 'Joan at Bog Eggs'.

John Greenwood was arrested, and he claimed to have received the unsigned note from 'Old Mike'. The latter took a little tracking down, but he was eventually arrested near Blackshawhead.

By this time the law had cast its net wide, and no fewer than seventeen people were being held along with 'Old Mike' on suspicion of the murder. However, the evidence against 'Joan at Bog Eggs' and 'Old Mike' was so strong that everyone else was released, and after appearing before a local magistrate they were committed to York Castle on February 18th. On the same day, Constable Wilson searched 'Old Mike's' house for the third time. He found concealed under a flag beneath the bed articles of cotton cloth and other goods. These were identified as belonging to Samuel Sutcliffe by his nephew, and a neighbour.

The trial of the two miscreants took place at York Castle on Friday, March 14th 1817. The charges were burglary and murder. Twenty-two witnesses from the district were taken to York. One of these witnesses, John Thomas of Midgley, said that he received a pair of shoes from John Greenwood on February 8th. These were produced and identified by Samuel's nephew, William Sutcliffe, as belonging to him and having been left at Hawden Hole.

Both prisoners told contradictory stories, each accusing the other as the instigator of the crime. 'Old Mike' said that Greenwood had asked him to come to Hawden Hole, that they had entered by a window and gone into the old man's room. When the old man had started up in bed they both ran away, and 'Old Mike' claimed that he never touched Samuel Sutcliffe.

John Greenwood's story was a little more complex, but it put all the blame on 'Old Mike'. Not only had the latter proposed the crime, but he had gone into the house while Greenwood stood outside. 'Old Mike' had brought out all the stolen goods to Greenwood, and then said that he had *taken the old man by the neck and was afraid he had killed him'*. In addition, Greenwood said that 'Old Mike' had given him a stolen gun to carry (one of the articles found by Constable Wilson at 'Old Mike's' house).

Character witnesses were called to testify on the good character of John Greenwood, and in his summing up the judge stated that all the evidence pointed to strangulation of Samuel Sutcliffe by 'Old Mike'. However, the judge stated that if the jury felt that the murder had been committed to prevent alarm, and to secure accomplishment of their design or robbing the house, then it was the duty of the jury to find *both* prisoners guilty.

The jury did not take long to find both prisoners guilty, and Greenwood fell on his knees protesting his innocence. However, the execution took place on Monday March 17th, when both prisoners were hanged, and their bodies delivered to surgeons for dissection.

THE HARDCASTLE CRAGS RAILWAY

A Growing Thirst - Between 1901 and 1908 a strange and wild breed of men descended upon Hardcastle Crags - the 'navvies'. Stranger still, a railway line was built up the valley along which steam engines ran! The 'navvy' invasion of 1901 was not the first one, nor yet the last, and the reason in every case was the growing thirst of the town of Halifax. As Halifax expanded into a large town during the nineteenth and twentieth centuries, the cry was for more and more drinking water for an ever-increasing population. The upper reaches of these local valleys, in the natural basins of the moorlands, made excellent sites for reservoirs, and so one was built at Widdop between 1871 and 1878.

The main problem was, of course, the transporting of men and materials to such remote spots. For the building of the Widdop reservoirs, a line was laid along the right-hand side of the river (looking up the valley) from the hillside below Pecket, and horses drew train loads of men and materials up to the Widdop site. This was known as Lipscombe's tram line, Lipscombe being the agent of Lord Savile, on whose land much of this work took place.

The most recent 'navvy invasion' came between 1927 and 1934 when the Gorple reservoirs were built. However, wedged between the first and the last was the one which in many ways was the most ambitious, and has left the most impressive evidence. This was the project of 1901 to 1908 which, in order to build reservoirs at Walshaw Dean, set out to create a steam railway up Hardcastle Crags.

The Walshaw Line - This ran from Whitehill Nook, below Heptonstall, up the left-hand side of the valley along the fields overlooking Hardcastle Crags. Tributary valleys descending into the Crags were crossed by wooden trestle bridges, and one of these was built at Clough Hole where the car-park near Greenwood Lee is now to be found.

Physical evidence of the existence of the line at the bottom end of the valley is hard to find. However, a drive for a mile or two along the Widdop Road from Clough Hole car-park, following the valley upwards, will alter this situation. Here we enter Blakedean, where the woods are replaced by rough pasture and moorland sweeping steeply down to the river. Looking down from the road one can clearly see a series of large, stone supports straddling the river. These impressive remains once carried a huge wooden trestle bridge which took the Hardcastle Crags Railway from the left-hand bank of the river to the right-hand bank, and hence the railway wound its way 'round the corner' and up the Walshaw valley. Flat shelves of land on both sides of the Hebden valley mark the course of the line in these upper reaches.

The Halifax Corporation financed this project, and the three foot

Silent outposts of the steam age at Blakedean

'Paddy Mails' on the trestle bridge at Blakedean

gauge railway ran five miles from Whitehill Nook to the Walshaw site. The Blakedean trestle bridge was 700 feet long and 105 feet high.

It apparently swayed slightly in strong winds, but it was stoutly built, and could take two engines with trucks laden with cement up to a weight of more than sixty tons. At time of writing, the 'Pack Horse' Inn, Blakedean, contains an interesting display of maps and photographs concerning the old lines and the Blakedean trestle bridge.

Dawson City and the 'Navvies' - It is difficult to imagine the impact of the Hardcastle Crags Railway on the 'locals'. No doubt some benefited through leasing their land for the line to run across, but how astonishing it must have seemed at first to have steam engines plying back and forth. How incredible to have the tranquillity of the valley shattered by the sounds and smells of clanking locomotives belching smoke and hissing steam! And when the novelty of all this had worn off, there were still the dreaded 'navvies' to contend with ...

The British 'navvy' or 'navigator' had become a name synonymous with hard work and heavy drinking since the great canal and railway building eras of the late eighteenth and nineteenth centuries. Enoch Tempest, a Manchester contractor, had won the tender for the job in June 1900, and he set up his headquarters at Whitehill Nook, Heptonstall. Here a hutted township was built to house the hundreds of 'navvies' who were employed first on building the line, and later the reservoirs. This became known as *Dawson City* as it was said that many of the 'navvies' on the job had worked on the Klondyke goldfields in Canada, and had lived in the original, more famous Dawson City.

Whitehall Nook, the site of *Dawson City*, is now simply a stretch of fields on the left-hand side as one takes the road from Slack Bottom which

A fearsome breed of men - "navvies" at Dawson City

bye-passes Heptonstall and descends towards Hebden Bridge. The fields, which can be seen between the left fork in the road at Slack Bottom and the sharp bend to the right lower down, offer a good, flat expanse of land, but otherwise there is no sign that this once was a township housing the ferocious 'navvies'.

The materials for the line and the reservoirs were hauled up the hillside from Hebden Bridge station to Dawson City by teams of horses and one steam lorry.

Horse power bringing steam power

Each locomotive used on the line needed as many as sixteen horses to drag it up the hillside on a sturdy wagon. Fifteen locomotives operated on the Hardcastle Crags Railway, and were maintained at a loco. shed at Dawson City.

The 'navvies' at *Dawson City* were a motley crew, including men who came from Yorkshire, Lancashire, Wales and Ireland. Men from the 'Emerald Isle' must have formed a strong contingent, however, for the engines which ran back and forth with the workers were known as *Paddy Mails*. The serenity and stillness of Hardcastle Crags would be rudely disturbed as the *Paddy Mails* left *Dawson City* at 5.30, 5.40 and 5.50 in the morning, packed with workers, and pulled by engines with a variety of names. *Robinson, Walton, Wade,* and *Parker* were named after Halifax town councillors. Another was named *Esau*; another *Walshaw Dean*; and yet another *Lipscombe*, after Lord Savile's agent.

The *Paddy Mails* returned at tea-time after the day's work was done. A hard day's work it must have been, for the 'navvies' were famed for their endurance, and these were the days of pick and shovel, when excavating

'Esau' - one of fifteen working in the wilderness

machinery was unheard of. Doubtless they were less safety conscious too, for there were several accidents on the line, and two fatalities. Winter must have been a trying time considering the exposed nature of the line, and it was often blocked by snow. The main task of the 'navvies' at times like these would be to keep the line open, and even to dig the engines out, for sometimes engines were lost in the snow for as long as three days!

The 'navvies' were known for working hard; they were also known for playing hard. After six days hard slog at the reservoir, they were ready for anything on a Saturday night. It was a matter of *'lock up your wives and daughters'* as the 'navvies' descended upon Heptonstall and Hebden Bridge for bouts of heavy drinking and fighting with the locals. The newspapers of the day contain a doleful catalogue of residents of *Dawson City* appearing before the local magistrates for a variety of offences associated with drunkenness and disorder. A religious mission was established at *Dawson City*, but even so, one of the chief diversions of the 'navvies' on Sundays seems to have been fighting among themselves.

Therefore, although the landlords of public houses may have thrived, no doubt many people breathed a sigh of relief when peace and quiet returned to the district on the departure of the 'navvies'. The first of the three Walshaw Dean reservoirs was opened in 1907, and the major part of the work was completed by 1908. The Hardcastle Crags Railway was used on a limited scale, however, until 1912. Then the Blakedean trestle bridge was demolished as unsafe; the line was taken up; and relative peace and tranquillity returned to Hardcastle Crags.

ACKNOWLEDGEMENTS

Much of the material in this book has been drawn from the booklet which I wrote in 1973 entitled 'Mill, Murder and Railway'.

Sources:-

1. An article on Greenwood Lee by H Kendall, Halifax Antiquarian Papers, 1917.

2. Articles on the Hardcastle Crags Railway and the Hawden Hole Murder by H Marshall, 'Hebden Bridge Times'.

3. 'The Slurring Rock Nature Trail', produced by Calderdale MBC.

4. The Longstaff Collection and the Hebden Bridge Literary and Scientific Society; both invaluable sources for photographs. Many thanks to Frank Woolrych for access to this material.

5. 'Halifax Evening Courier' for line drawing on front cover, by Alan Jones.

6. Calderdale Central Reference Library for photocopy of banknote, HT - p332.

7. Bob Dobson of Landy Publishing, Blackpool for help and advice.

8. Louise K. Thomas for photographs not otherwise acknowledged and Gibson family tree.

9. Emma Thomas for word-processing.